Three Cheers for Mother Jones!

illustrated by
Kathleen Garry-McCord

Holt, Rinehart and Winston / New York

THREE
CHEERS for
MOTHER JONES!

by Jean Bethell

Library of Congress Cataloging in Publication Data

Bethell, Jean.   Three Cheers for Mother Jones!
SUMMARY: Retells, from the point of view of
one of the participants, the story of Mother Jones'
famous children's march in 1903 made to protest
working conditions for children.
   1.   Children—Employment—United States—History
—Juvenile literature—Pictorial works.
2.   Jones, Mary Harris, 1830-1930.   3.   Strikes
and lockouts—Textile industry—Pennsylvania—
Philadelphia—History—Juvenile literature—
Pictorial works.   [1.   Children—Employment.
2.   Jones, Mary Harris, 1830-1930]   I.   Garry-McCord,
Kathleen.   II.   Title.   HD6247.T42U62
331.88'092'4   [B]   79-28655   ISBN 0-03-054831-4

Contents

Chapter 1

My Name is James

Philadelphia, Pa., November 1903

This is my sister, Emmy.
She's only seven years old.
We work here in this dirty old mill.
It's the worst job in the world.

We work twelve hours a day.
We don't go to school.
We never get out in the sun.
We're tired all the time.
Sometimes we have accidents and get hurt.
They pay us two dollars a week.

That's Father over there.
He gets thirteen dollars a week.
Our family can't live on that.
That's why Emmy and I have to work.
We hate it.
Everybody who works here hates it.

We hate the owner, too. He's mean,
and he doesn't pay us enough.
He gets rich and we stay poor.
We don't think that's fair.

Chapter 2

Here Comes Mother Jones

Philadelphia, Pa., June 1903

Last summer we tried to do
something about it.
We went to see the owner.
"Please raise our pay," said Father,
"so our kids won't have to work."
"We want to go to school," I said.
But he wouldn't listen.
"Get back to work or I'll fire you!"

That made us mad.
So we walked out.
We all went out on strike!
We walked around in front of the mill.
We waited for the owner to offer us
more money.

Then a lady called Mother Jones came to
the mill. She was old—as old as my
grandma. But she had a lot of spunk.
She shook her fist at the mill owner.
"Shame on you!" she said.
"Hiring babies to do men's work."

"Hooray for Mother Jones!" we shouted.

"Set these children free!" she cried.
"Give their parents enough to live on!"

"Never!" said the mill owner.

"Then we'll go see the President!"
said Mother Jones.

"What can he do?" asked Father.
"Can he raise our pay? Can he keep
our children out of the mills?"
"Let's find out," said Mother Jones.
"Let's ask him for help. That's what
presidents are for—to help people."

"Hooray!" we shouted.
"Let's all go see the President!"

Chapter 3

The Long March Begins

Philadelphia, Pa., July 7, 1903

There was a big story in the paper
about our march.
Everybody in town came to see us off.

Mother Jones led the parade.
Father and I were right behind her. And about
two hundred people were right behind us.
Emmy wanted to come, but she was too young.
She stayed home with our mother and the baby.

What fun we had! Music played.
People cheered. And away we went.
Hup-two-three-four!

We had a long way to go. The
President was at his summer home,
125 miles away.
Hup-two-three-four!
We didn't care how far it was. We were
so glad to be out of that dirty old mill.

Along the way people gave us water
and food. We ate lunch while we walked.
The day was hot, and after a while
we began to slow down. Mother Jones
looked tired. I helped her into a cart.
She let the small children ride with her.

By four o'clock we had to stop.
We lay down in a field to rest.

"We'll spend the night here,"
said Mother Jones.
I helped the men put up the tents.
After dinner we talked and sang.
Father fell asleep.
I sat up for a long time, looking
at the stars. I was happy. I didn't
want to go back to the mill, ever.

Chapter 4

We Run into Trouble

Pennsylvania, July 8–10, 1903

The next day was very hot. The sun
burned us. We walked slower and slower.
People were getting sick.
"We quit!" said some of them."It's too hot."
Lots of them turned around and went home.

At the end of the second day there were
only a hundred marchers left.
"Don't give up," Mother Jones said.
"We still have a long way to go."

The third day it rained. The roads
turned to mud. The carts got stuck.
I helped the men pull them out.

Then the bugs came. They buzzed
and stung and drove us crazy.
More people went home.

The next day, Father hurt his foot.
He could hardly walk.
"Let's go home," he said.
"Please let me stay," I begged.
"I want to see the President."
"All right, son. Good luck," he said,
and gave me a hug.

Mother Jones smiled at me.
"That's the spirit, James. Stick with it."
"Yes ma'am," I said. "If you can make it,
so can I."

Chapter 5

Marching Across New Jersey

New Jersey, July 11–23, 1903

When we crossed the bridge to New Jersey,
there were only sixty of us left.
"You're doing fine!" said Mother Jones.

On and on we went, day after day.
We stopped in many towns.
Mother Jones made a speech in each place.
We passed a hat around and people
put money in it.

Our march was getting famous.
The newspapers called it
"The March of the Mill Children."

One night we slept in a hotel.
I never saw a hotel before. I liked it.
I had a whole bed to myself!
But most nights we slept in fields
or empty buildings.

I was tired and dirty, but I didn't care.
I was going to see the President.
Maybe he would shake my hand!

We kept on walking. Then we came
to the Hudson River. We could see
New York City on the other side.
We could hardly wait to get there.

Chapter 6

New York, at Last

July 23, 1903

We went across the river on a
big boat. It was such fun.
I wanted to stay on the boat all day.

At last we were in New York.
What a place!
All those people.
All those tall buildings.
All that *noise*!

"Stop!" said the police.
"You can't march here!"
I was scared.

"Nonsense!" said Mother Jones.
"We'll go ask the Mayor."

"You must let us march, Mr. Mayor.
We're trying to help these poor children."
"Go right ahead," said the Mayor.
"I love parades!"

It was a fine, big parade.
Many people came to see us.
Mother Jones put me up on the stage.
"Look at this poor lad.
He has to work in the mill
so he can buy food."

"I want to go to school," I said.
"I want to learn to read and write."
The people cheered.

Next day there was a story about me
in the paper. Mother Jones read it to me.
My family would be proud.

Chapter 7

A Trip to Coney Island

Coney Island, N.Y., July 27, 1903

Our next stop was Coney Island.
We walked on the beach.
We saw a wild animal show.
That night, when Mother Jones made
her speech, we got into some empty cages.
We roared like animals and shook the bars.

"See these poor children?" she said.
"Trapped in the mills like animals
trapped in cages. Child labor is a crime.
We must change the laws.
Theodore Roosevelt, here we come!"

Chapter 8

The President's Summer Home

Oyster Bay, N.Y., July 29, 1903

Mother Jones took five of us to
see the President.
I wondered what Mr. Roosevelt would
say to me.

Then we were at the gate.
We could see his big house
at the top of the hill.
Some of his children were playing
on the lawn.
"They're lucky," said Mother Jones.
"They don't have to work in the mills."

Two men came to the gate. "Mother Jones?"
they said. "The President will not be able
to see you."
Mother Jones was shocked.
"He won't see us? We've marched for
twenty-two days. And now he won't see us?"
"Sorry, madam. Mr. Roosevelt says
he can't help you."

"I'm sorry, children," said Mother Jones.
"Don't feel bad," I told her.
"We did our best."
But she felt very bad. And so did I.
I didn't want to work in the mill.

It was all over. Our march had failed.
We took the train back home.

Chapter 9

Back to Work at the Mill

Philadelphia, Pa., November 1903

And here I am, back at the same old job.
Emmy and I still get two dollars a week.
It's still noisy and dirty.
We still hate it.

But listen! What's that?
People are cheering.

It's Mother Jones! She's back!

"I have good news for you," she says.
"Our march didn't fail, after all.
The governor is going to help us!"

"Hooray! Hooray!
Three cheers for Mother Jones!"

"Someday the laws will be changed,"
she tells us. "Someday things
will be better for all of you."

Father and Emmy and I are glad to
hear that. Now we have something
to hope for.

A Note from the Author

There really was a Mother Jones. She spent her whole life trying to make things better for American workers, young and old.

In 1903, at the time of this story, there were over one million boys and girls under fourteen who worked in mines, mills, and factories.

It was hard, dangerous work. Some got lung disease from breathing the black dust in coal mines or the lint-filled air of textile mills. Many were crippled when their fingers or hands got caught in the machinery. And perhaps worst of all, these children never had a chance to go to school—they grew up not knowing how to read or write.

From 1870 to 1930, Mary Harris Jones fought for decent wages and healthy working conditions. She traveled from coal mines in West Virginia to Colorado copper mines to textile mills in Pennsylvania and Alabama, holding rallies, making speeches, urging the workers to band together for their own good. She was our country's first woman labor organizer.

Mother Jones was seventy-three when she led the Children's Crusade to see President Theodore Roosevelt. Although he was against child labor, he could not persuade Congress to pass a federal law making it illegal. Another thirty-five years went by before such a law was finally enacted.

But the long, difficult march of the mill children was not entirely in vain. This is what Mother Jones says about it in her autobiography:

> We had drawn the attention of the nation to the crime of child labor. And while the strike of the textile workers was lost and the children driven back to work, not long afterward the Pennsylvania legislature passed a child labor law that sent thousands of children home from the mills and kept thousands of others from entering the factory until they were fourteen years of age.

About the Author

Jean Bethell has written thirty children's books, including *Bathtime* and the coming *Playmates*. She lives in New York City and works as a librarian at the Center for Medical Consumers.

About the Illustrator

Kathleen Garry-McCord is a free-lance illustrator. She has illustrated *A Pebble in Newcomb's Pond* by Marianna Dengler, and is a resident of Southern California.